Oscar Fay Adams, Horatio Nelson Powers

Lyrics of the Hudson

Oscar Fay Adams, Horatio Nelson Powers

Lyrics of the Hudson

ISBN/EAN: 9783744795340

Printed in Europe, USA, Canada, Australia, Japan

Cover: Foto ©Thomas Meinert / pixelio.de

More available books at **www.hansebooks.com**

LYRICS OF THE HUDSON

POEMS

BY

HORATIO NELSON POWERS

AUTHOR OF "TEN YEARS OF SONG," "THROUGH THE YEAR,"
"POEMS EARLY AND LATE"

WITH MEMORIAL INTRODUCTION BY

OSCAR FAY ADAMS

BOSTON
D. LOTHROP COMPANY
WASHINGTON STREET OPPOSITE BROMFIELD

PREFACE.

It is with a feeling closely akin to pain that one takes up the work of an author very lately gone from among men. It is like entering the room of a friend when the friend has just quitted it forever. There are his books in the same order as when he left them : the waste basket still holds its litter of pamphlets and torn papers ; the desk is strewn with letters and manuscripts ; the pen yet lies where it fell from the tired fingers of its owner across the half-completed page. So with the book that comes to us soon after the death of its author, the book that he had planned and never saw. Perhaps the proof-sheets came to him day after day as he felt life slipping away from him, wondering perchance, as his hold on material things relaxed, if he should ever see the closing pages. Or possibly the summons came suddenly, and he in obedience to it

> *" At its topmost speed let fall the pen
> And left the tale half-told."*

The larger number of the poems which compose the present volume were written by the author in the last four years of his life, and his intention, confided to a few friends, was to have published them privately as a surprise prepared for the wife whose love had been the inspiration of his pen for so many years. But his was not to be the hand which was to offer her this token of affection, for before any active steps had been taken regarding publication he had done with time. It has been thought best by those nearest to him that the poems which represent, in verse at least, his latest thought, should not be withheld from circulation, but given to the world in permanent form, accompanied with some few words concerning him. These few words it has fallen to me, as one of those who loved him and whom he loved, to supply.

Horatio Nelson Powers was born of old Dutch ancestry, in Amenia, Dutchess County, N. Y., on the thirtieth of April, 1826. His education was obtained at the Amenia Seminary and at Union College, from which he was graduated in 1850. After graduation he spent two years in teaching and subsequently entering the General Theological Seminary of the Episcopal Church, was graduated from that institution in 1855. He was ordained by Bishop Horatio Potter in that year, and for the next two years served as assistant minister in St. James' Church, at Lancaster, Penn.

While living at Lancaster he was married to Clémence Emma, daughter of the late Professor Francis Favel-Gouraud of the University of Paris. From Lancaster he removed to Davenport, Iowa, where he remained in charge of a parish for eleven years, serving for a portion of that time as President of Griswold College. While at Davenport he received from Union College the degree of D. D. In 1868 he accepted a call to the rectorship of St. John's Church in Chicago, and in 1875 removed from Chicago to Bridgeport, Conn., where he became rector of Christ Church. In this position he continued for ten years, leaving Bridgeport in 1885. A year later he was asked to take charge of a church at Sparkill, N. Y., which he consented to do, making his home in the adjoining village of Piermont-on-the-Hudson, a choice determined mainly by the beauty of the surrounding country. Except for six months spent in Europe in 1890 he was never afterward absent from Piermont longer than for a few days at a time. Always a sincere lover of nature he found in this quiet spot on the hillside overlooking the broad Tappan Zee the realization of many of his dreams. From his rectory windows the prospect was one in which his soul could daily take the most intense delight and satisfaction.

"*How little I anticipated such a retreat as this I have been graciously led to without any plan of my own,*" *he once said to me. Deeper and deeper the peace and joy of this new home sank into his heart till he could write to me in early June of* 1887 : "*I never was so happy in all my life before. So many birds singing and singing; such a wealth of blossoms and tender skies, such a magnificence of landscape instinct with the divine breath, such peace of heart, such a sweet atmosphere of love in my little church — it seemed that I was enjoying a perpetual benediction! I have never known such blessed restfulness and tranquillity as in this retreat along the hills of Piermont. I have known sorrow year after year, I have had continual solicitude and troubles, but they have not killed my faith, hope and charity. Now I am reaping the invisible harvest of the heart — am actually 'living before I die.'*"

It was here at Piermont on the morning of September 6, 1890, *that his life ended on the banks of the same river where it began, sixty-four years earlier.*

In 1875 *a volume of his religious essays entitled* Through the Year, *was published, and in* 1876 *his first volume of verse,* Poems, Early and Late, *appeared. A second was published in* 1887 *with the title* Ten

Years of Song. Dr. Powers wrote much for the press, his poems and essays appearing in nearly all the prominent periodicals of the country. He was deeply interested in art as well as literature, and was for some years the American correspondent of L'Art. To him Philip Gilbert Hamerton dedicated his book, The Unknown River, and for many years the two men were in constant correspondence, although they never met. He was peculiarly happy in his friendships, and beside the intimate acquaintance with Bryant and Bayard Taylor which he possessed he knew well many other literary men of his time. He gave his whole self in his friendships, keeping nothing back from the value of the gift, and so the welfare of those whom he loved was very much to him. "There is no good I do not wish you," he writes to me at one time. It was my happy privilege to stand closer to him than some others whom he knew, but his interest in each of his friends was always generous, abundant and sincere. In a very real sense he bore their burdens with his own and rejoiced when they made merry.

Of his poetry it is not needful to speak critically here. A quiet meditative optimism is its dominant note, the optimism of a nature that with its first enthusiasms tempered by many phases of subsequent experience still remains sure that past all doubting "good is yet the final goal." To read it is to enter into spiritual communion with one whose thoughts are as " the benediction that follows after prayer." But to have known the writer in his bodily presence is to have felt that same benediction strike deep down among all the fibers of one's mortal being.

> *Death hath no power o'er such as he :*
> *The fullness of the life to be*
> *Shone round him in the life he spent*
> *Within the body's prison pent.*
> *Texts might we gather from his looks,*
> *Such as men read in holy books,*
> *And through his words could hear at will*
> *The Master's gracious accents still.*

OSCAR FAY ADAMS.

Felton Hall,
   Cambridge, Mass.
      Lent, 1891.

CONTENTS.

CONTENTS.

LYRICS OF THE HUDSON.

LYRICS OF THE HUDSON.

THE HILLS OF PIERMONT.

A SONG.

O HAPPY hills of Piermont,
  How fair ye stand to-day,
The May sun on your slopes of green,
  Your woods with blossoms gay !
How tenderly the thrushes sing,
  How soft the breezes blow !
Blue, blue the sky — the apple-trees
  With fragrance overflow.

O blooming hills of Piermont,
  How sweetly ye look down
On the far-flashing Hudson
  And many a little town !

How fondly on your loveliness
    Gaze those who sadly roam,
And long, in your bewitching charm
    For such a sheltered home!

O lovely hills of Piermont,
    How blessed your repose!
How in the hearts that love ye
    Your own contentment grows!
Your bosky steeps and garden walks
    With soulful dreams are dear,
And a benignant spirit broods
    In all your atmosphere.

O happy hearths of Piermont,
    How restfully ye stand,
Safe in the shadow of a rock
    Above a peaceful land!
Where, to the raptured vision, spreads
    Another realm so fair?
And where, amid her templed hills,
    Is Nature more at prayer?

O noble hills of Piermont,
   How rich your charms to-day!
Ne'er dawned upon your gracious slopes
   A more enchanting May.
Your fountains gush, your robins sing,
   Your scented breezes play;
The great world thunders on — but, ah!
   How far it seems away!

NYACK.

HERE the great river sweeps
  Royal, broad-breasted;
Here the dark headland keeps
  Watch unmolested;
Here bask, in tangles green,
  Slopes flower-sprinkled;
Gapes here the weird ravine
  Rock-split and wrinkled.

Grander the forests grow,
  Coaxing your ramble;
Lovely the scene below
  Where the waves gambol;
Where the far landscape's line
  Fades soft and tender,
And the fair villas shine
  In the sun's splendor.

Snug 'neath the mountain's shield
  Nestles the village,
Bright as a jeweled field
  Tempting to pillage.
Homes that through joyous days
  Love's arm incloses;
Bloom-broidered lawns, and ways
  Lighted with roses.

Fadeless the picture rare —
  Ah, my lips falter! —
Hung in the sacred air
  O'er the heart's altar.
How it calms, how it tells
  Its soul-haunting story,
Like the chiming of bells
  In eventide's glory!

A ROCKLAND SUNSET.

THE summer storm has passed, and, all at
    once,
The sinking sun breaks through the leaden
    gloom,
And floods the vast expanse of mount and vale
With an exceeding glory. Here I stand,
On the abutment of the Palisades —
That mighty wall along the Hudson's marge —
Its utmost northern precipice sublime —
And scan the splendid prospect, as the change
Grows rich in heaven and earth of gleaming
    sky,
And shining mountain top, and fields ablaze
With yellow flame, and Tappan Zee asleep
In warm effulgence. Here, elate, I watch
The miracle of beauty as, behind
The hills of Ramapo that girt the west

With royal purple, the great sun goes down,
And rifts of cloud, here banked in giant shapes,
And there in flocks soft, tremulous, inspired,
Gather, and break, and melt in tender fires,
That make the pageant of the skies divine.

It is a host of billows rosy fringed,
Tumbling upon a paradise of flowers.
It is a cataract of flame, now fixed
Amid ethereal precipices,
Then dashing crimson tides on saffron shores
And mingling with an opalescent sea.
It is a pomp of banners waved on walls
Of porphyry and amber, floating wide
O'er gardens where the angels weave their
      crowns.
Ah! how the glory changes; — mighty folds
Of luminous tapestry flung afar,
Shot through with feathery splendor, broidered
      wide
With dark carnations — belts of golden green
Between the pink horizon and the wastes

Of intense radiance of the higher heavens —
Mountains of bloom that heave, and split, and
    glow
Showering the petals of celestial flowers
On meadows soft with verdure, on old woods,
The Hudson's tranquil breast, and Hook's still
    dome,
Set like a jewel on earth's happy brow.
The pageant fades and, steep by steep, dis-
    solve
The airy cliffs, furrows of rose and gold
That ploughed the dazzling fields of upper air,
Pinnacle and buttress of the gorgeous shapes
That hung in heaven and caught its mystery,
And dim grow all the vales, and on the hills
Of the enchanted river dies the day,
And solemn twilight sheds on all repose.

MY WALK TO CHURCH.

BREATHING the summer-scented air
  Along the bowery mountain way,
Each Lord's-day morning I repair
  To serve my church, a mile away.

Below, the glorious river lies —
  A bright broad-breasted, sylvan sea —
And round the sumptuous highlands rise,
  Fair as the hills of Galilee.

Young flowers are in my path.   I hear
  Music of unrecorded tone.
The heart of Beauty beats so near,
  Its pulses modulate my own.

The shadow on the meadow's breast
  Is not more calm than my repose

As, step by step, I am the guest
　　Of every living thing that grows.

Ah, something melts along the sky,
　　And something rises from the ground,
And fills the inner ear and eye
　　Beyond the sense of sight and sound.

It is not that I strive to see
　　What Love in lovely shapes has wrought —
Its gracious messages to me
　　Come, like the gentle dews, unsought.

I merely walk with open heart
　　Which feels the secret in the sign;
But, O, how large and rich my part
　　In all that makes the feast divine!

Sometimes I hear the happy birds
　　That sang to Christ beyond the sea,
And softly His consoling words
　　Blend with their joyous minstrelsy.

Sometimes in royal vesture glow
  The lilies that He called so fair,
Which never toil nor spin, yet show
  The loving Father's tender care.

And then along the fragrant hills
  A radiant presence seems to move,
And earth grows fairer as it fills
  The very air I breathe with love.

And now I see one perfect face,
  And hastening to my church's door,
Find Him within the holy place
  Who, all my way, went on before.

ROCKLAND.

A REALM of beauty! Softly sloping hills
　And noble heights embowered in luscious
　　green,
Wide, flower-sown meadows etched with silver
　　rills,
　And grand old groves with dusky glens
　　between;
Thickets where sing the thrushes all the day
　By springs that gush 'neath tangled fern
　　and vine,
Sweet pastures, orchards, vineyards, gardens
　　gay —
　All in one lovely picture here combine.

The Hudson, like a royal sea, rolls by,
　Along a Paradise that ages made,
Where in delicious nooks fair homesteads lie,
　And stands on guard the giant Palisade!

Set like a gem divinely smiles the lake
  In calms of moonshine, and at evening's
    glow,
And what a witchery its features take
  When myriad lilies fringe its breast with
    snow.

And when the autumn comes in splendid
    might,
  Like him of Bozrah, what a glory runs
O'er wood and copse and mead and leafy
    height,
  Rich as the blazonry of setting suns.
And, in the wintry days, what wreaths are flung
  Of silvery plumage o'er the landscape bare,
What diamond garlands through the groves
    are strung,
  That drive the cunning craftsman to despair!

Magnificent in aspect, thou art strong!
  Thy softest charms on living rock repose,

And he who scorns does mystic Nature wrong,
  Nor yet the secret power of beauty knows.
Fling out thy royal splendors, rock-ribbed
    land !
  The flower of granite is the flower most fair.
On solid truth benignant lives expand,
  And glorious is the loveliness they wear.

SPRING WEATHER.

HEAR the bird in the wood,
 Where, from sheaths gently torn,
 Silken leaflets are born,
 On this exquisite morn,
In the spring weather;
Is it not very good —
 This song of the bird
And May-morn together?
 This welcoming bird
And the soft spring weather?

See the white gauze of shad-blows
 In the grove's sunny places,
 Like faint silvery laces
 O'er vanishing faces,
In the spring weather;
How the witchery grows,

With the blossoms song-kissed —
Bird and bloom flung together —
The music and bloom-mist,
And amber-stained weather.

Feel the spirit that steals
Dainty sweets everywhere,
Of the earth and the air,
As your prodigal share
Of the spring weather;
How it hallows and heals!
Bathes heart in its rapture —
Bird, bloom, love together —
O the sweet, silent rapture
Of the soul of spring weather!

A MAY CAROL.

WHAT now is Love doing?
Ah, watch, as the buds burst, as the grasses
    are feeling
The mist and the sunshine, and green things
    are stealing
Fond glances at skies that are sweetly reveal-
    ing
A tremulous tenderness holy and healing ;
Feel the witchery haunting the luminous
    places
In meadow and glen, where faint, flowery
    faces,
With the delicate charm of their infantile
    graces,
Are so coy in their greetings, and the brook
    races —

A ripple of rapture — o'er mosses and patches
Of silver that brighten, and all the air catches
The luster and calm of a Spirit that's wooing
Life out of life, and earth's glory renewing —
A beauty more dear in one's passionate view-
　　ing —
　　　And this Love is doing !

　　　What now is Love saying ?
Just put your ear close to the herbage that's
　　springing,
To the vine that is happy in climbing and
　　clinging ;
List, as the birds are caressing and singing
Mid the odors and tints that the season is
　　bringing ;
Lie at noon in the woods, or as sunlight is
　　waning —
The murmurs you hear are of praise, not
　　complaining.
Even silence is voiceful. The soul that is
　　reigning

Is beauty enrobing.   The breathings that kiss
    you
Are the life in the soil, and the sap, and the
    tissue
From a corpuscle's stir to the chorus of ocean,
The tones that entrance are the music of
    motion.
On the harp of the Infinite, Goodness is
    playing :
" If you love me, dear heart, go a-Maying,
    a-Maying " —
    And this Love is saying !

UNDER THE SNOW.

Musing, across the still, white fields
    And frozen forest wastes, I go,
And hear, as in a dream, the tones
    Of life and love beneath the snow.

Something is telling me of days
    Sweet with fresh scents and mating birds,
When earth's impassioned heart shall speak
    A tenderer eloquence than words.

E'en now the glee of seeds that break
    Their vernal sepulcher, I hear;
And laugh of bursting buds and whirr
    Of radiant wings are in my ear.

I hear innumerable leaves,
    Æolian idyls far away,

And faint, low ditties in the dells,
   And what the myriad grasses say.

Ah, sweet as love the cowslip's breath !
   But sweeter on my spirit falls
The poem the arbutus sends,
   As breathed upon her mountain walls.

I hear it, and the lily's lips
   Warm with the South's caressing air.
The chorus deepens — spring's dear sounds
   Are floating round me everywhere,

The far-off talk of odorous trees,
   The lisping of the meadow stream,
The coo of doves, the sprouting grain,
   And dreams the apple-blossoms dream ;

And children culling in their play
   The flowers they waste and know not why,
Prattling and chirping, as they feel
   A joy for which their elders sigh ;

And strains that from the earth arise,
  As o'er the misty landscape flows
The golden sunshine, and in heaven
  The rainbow's splendid symbol glows.

Entranced I muse, till, in my May,
  I walk again with one most dear,
And life's cold snows and icy paths
  In youth's high visions, disappear.

A RURAL CHURCH.

Nesting mid vines and leafage, where the
  lawn
  Slopes toward a softly-lingering valley
    stream,
The little church hides, like a soul withdrawn
  From the world's noise to worship and to
    dream.

Simple the cool gray pile, embowered in green,
  With every charm that modesty can yield,
As one of winning face and artless mien
  Is lovelier still with features half-concealed.

Near by are sumptuous hills, and lordly trees
  Their summits crown and fringe the pools
    below,
Where, under their majestic canopies,
  Daisies and golden-hearted lilies blow.

It is the Sabbath, and the summer morn
　Is sweet with flowers, and birds, and new-
　　　mown hay, —
As if a spirit breathed, and life new born
　Blossomed in all that glorifies the day.

Within, the church is redolent with blooms
　Fresh from the fields whose orisons they
　　　bear:
God's peace is on them, and their smile
　　　relumes
　The hopes of hearts aweary with their care.

O sacred hour! the vain world far away!
　Doth He not hear who marks the sparrow's
　　　fall?
How good it seems in this dear place to stay,
　Musing on Love that filleth all in all!

Sometimes, in concert with the sacred song,
　A thrush's trill floats in upon the air;
Sometimes, a breeze wafts, with its sweets,
　　　along
　The purer fragrance of the breath of prayer.

DISQUIETED.

THE winds are hushed, the river sleeps,
   The moon shines soft and bright,
And still a shudder through you creeps
   At something out of sight.

What is it through the scented gloom
   Breathes such a strange unrest,
And mid voluptuous summer bloom
   Haunts your unquiet breast ?

You feel it when the sweetest things
   Your finest senses greet,
When with full hands Love freely flings
   Her lilies at your feet.

Beyond the veil you strain to see,
   Though all earth's charms beguile,

And wonder what your lot will be
  After a little while, —

After your gains, and joys, and tears,
  After your tasks are done,
And all your swiftly flying years
  End with your goal unwon !

A PRESENCE.

Something stirs in the grass,
   Something dimples the stream,
And I feel its breath pass,
   Like a kiss in a dream.

It is here in the vine,
   It is there on the sea,
And it flings out its sign
   Where clouds frolic and flee.

It trembles in sunlight,
   It pictures the ground,
'Tis the magic of sight,
   'Tis the palace of sound.

It bides where the bird flies, —
   In its nest and its note,

Where sweet echo replies,
  And the fireflies float.

Round the dewdrop it folds,
  And the jewels of frost;
Not an atom it holds
  From its bosom is lost.

In the cleft of the rock,
  On the pansy's warm breast,
In the tempest's fierce shock,
  On the wild billow's crest,

In flame and in thunder,
  In birth and in death,
In laughter and wonder,
  Flows the tide of its breath.

Ah, the scenes it incloses!
  It is moistened with tears;
It colors the roses
  Of bridals and biers.

It hears all that's spoken,
   It holds all that's fair,
In vain bread is broken,
   Lest its Presence is there.

ON OCCUPYING A NEW HOUSE.

We fear and we rejoice.
  In awe, we pause before
The portal, for a Voice
  Austere is at the door.

" The sad past leave behind —
  The world's mad strife and din ;
A grateful, quiet mind,
  And sunny faiths bring in.

" Keep sweet this atmosphere
  For Love's unruffled tone ;
Give pallid Want good cheer,
  And Modesty a throne.

" Grief shall be thine and pain —
  From these no house is free ;

But let naught churlish stain
  The robes of Charity.

" Life here shall poems breathe
  That hallow every room,
And on the threshold leave
  A heavenly perfume,

" Or noxious vapors spread
  On hearth and hall and stair,
Till later dwellers dread
  The feeling in the air !

" As thou art, it shall be
  To wife and child and guest ;
An inn of low degree,
  Or Love's ambrosial nest."

HYMN.

O Lord, our souls revive :
   They languish low and faint.
In vain we seek to shrive
   Their guiltiness and taint.

We look to Thee and pray ;
   To Thee we humbly cling ;
May we abide alway
   Beneath thy shelt'ring wing.

Keep us, O Lord, from sin ;
   Hold us by Thy right hand ;
Impart Thy strength within,
   And we shall surely stand.

We wait for Thine own breath
   Upon our hearts to blow.
O conqueror of death !
   Thy life to us bestow.

THE NAMELESS COURIER OF
CONEMAUGH.

On noble charger strong and fleet,
A rider speeds through Johnstown's street,
Whose voice the very welkin thrills —
" For life, dear life, fly to the hills !
Haste, haste ! death smites, if you delay,
Fly to the hills — away, away ! "
He dashes on — his foaming steed
Is like the wind.   O will they heed?
Wilder his cry, his goal unwon,
And still he shouts and thunders on —
" The hills ; the hills ! " the people stare :
Is this a maniac riding there?

O God in heaven !   With sudden break
Plunges the mighty mountain lake —
Its barrier burst — with headlong fall,

Through rended gorge and ragged wall,
Down, down, to happy vales below —
O utter, helpless, hopeless woe!

A roar! as if earth's heart strings broke
By some Cyclopean thunder-stroke,
A quaking of the rock-ribbed hills
That all the air with anguish fills.
It comes! it comes — the falling sea,
Mad with its own immensity,
Terrific with its load of doom —
A city's death! a city's tomb!

Down, down it leaps and roars and raves;
A monster fed with groans and graves!
Insatiate throat, fast gulping down
The quiet farm, the little town,
The fair, the brave, the good, the wise —
O horrid, guilty sacrifice!

"The hills, the hills," — but faint his tone
Who rides so desperately alone:

Too late !   The avalanche's blow
Crushes the city crouched below —
A maelstrom now, where corpses sail
Tossing torn limbs and faces pale,
And then a fiery jail —a sea
Of ghastly, crisp humanity.

Oh, fell he nobly in the race
To warn the careless burgh apace.
Struck by the high and hissing wave —
His dying breath a cry to save.
O hero, in a cause more true
Than ever old Crusader knew;

Nameless, thy deed's tremendous power,
Faithful in danger's fatal hour,
Shall awe and fire with holy rage
The hearts of men from age to age,
And tell, bright laureled names beside,
Of one who for the people died.

A DEATHLESS VOICE.

ABOVE the sobbing of a stricken nation
    O'er her great chieftain murdered in his
        prime ;
Above melodious bursts of lamentation
    That make earth's sorrow awful and sublime,

I hear a voice from deeps serene, supernal,
    Stifling the heart-break of a world in tears :
He speaks whose fame is spotless and eternal :
    O, hear and heed, ye who to hear have ears !

" Mourn not for me with aimless, nerveless
        sorrow ;
    I only was the vessel used to hold
The treasure lavished for a better morrow
    Whose dawn already tints the hills with gold.

46

" All that I was in deed and aspiration,
    In steadfast purpose and supreme desire,
I left upon the altar of the Nation —
    By Love bestowed and fuel for its fire.

" Look past the instrument that now is broken,
    To Him who touched its quick, responsive
        strings ;
Hear Him who through the fruitful years has
        spoken
    The quick'ning truth that makes men priests
        and kings.

" With chastened hearts accept the revelation
    That righteous service is the noblest good.
Ye build in vain, save on the firm foundation
    Of Honor's rock and Duty's hardihood.

" All glory is a phantom thin and fleeting
    That is not of the spirit pure and strong.
O brethren ! speed the grand angelic greeting,
    ' Good will to men,' and dies each hateful
        wrong.

" Rise on the faith that makes the people
    dearer,
  Clasp hands in deeds that trampled right
    befriend,
Welcome the touch that brings the nations
    nearer,
  And Freedom's mighty empire shall not
    end."

THE WONDERFUL.

IF thou art seeking loveliness more sweet
   Than e'er to craving hearts of old was given,
Faint with thy quest, though once thy steps
     were fleet,
   Come see the face that is most loved in
     heaven.

'Tis not a burning spirit of the Lord,
   Leading the tuneful host with seraph lyre,
Nor mighty cherub, whose high deeds accord
   With flaming measures of the starry choir.

'Tis not a beauteous soul that, near the throne,
   In rapture of uncounted years has dwelt,
Until the beauty brooded on has grown
   Into the life its joy so long has felt.

Come, but with heart whose simple lowlihood
   Asks only that its vision may be clear;
Come with the meekness that receives the good
   For its own sake, however it appear.

It is a babe new-born, turn not away;
   Ah, thou art smitten by the Wonder shown!
Here is the sun that ushers earth's great day,
   Here is the monarch of an endless throne.

Gaze on entranced — all thou hast sought is
     here —
   Thy dream of perfect life — its seal and
     sign —
All that can ravish soul, make being dear;
   Come, take the gift — all thou canst take, is
     thine,

Only a babe! yet here is regnant power,
   The charm that wins the nations yet to be,
The crown and joy of man's consummate
     flower,
   The freedom in which one is truly free.

Only a babe ! but see how hearths grow bright,
   And Wrong is smitten in his baleful lair,
And fade the horrid shapes that haunt the
     night,
   And Truth leaps forth, and dies the fiend
     Despair.

Serene, in that poor, barren manger-bed,
   The wondrous Child in nature's weakness
     lies ;
But from that fount the light of life is shed,
   A new world joins the chorus of the skies.

The heaven of heaven to lowest earth de-
     scends,
   Beats now the heart of God in human veins,
The age of wrath and hateful error ends,
   The Prince of Peace o'er love's broad em-
     pire reigns.

WHITSUN-DAY.

O Light of Light eternal!
    Sole Sun of every sphere!
O gifts of life supernal!
    The very God is here!

His heart is overflowing:
    Signs blaze in every land:
The heights and depths are showing
    His unexhausted hand.

Dear soul of eager yearning,
    Salute the tongues of fire!
The chaff of earth is burning,
    Foul shapes of wrong expire.

How bloom the desert places!
    Down crash strongholds of sin!

Peace on transfigured faces
   Reveals the Christ within.

From weakness, woe and weeping,
   The white-robed victors come ;
The halt and maimed are leaping ;
   And shout the blind and dumb.

O sea of love unbounded !
   O heaven of sinless breath !
Ne'er shall that sea be sounded,
   That heaven o'ercast with death.

I bask in light whose splendor
   The farthest star-mists own ;
I feel arms strong and tender
   That round the worlds are thrown.

I enter where the roses
   Of sweetest crowns are flung,
I rest where One discloses
   A glory yet unsung.

Deep after deep, forever,
  The gates of life unfold!
Sing, happy heart! For never
  Shall life and love grow old.

ANNIE.

1875–76.

THE sudden sorrow smote us so,
　With numbing pain, confusing all,
At first we did not fully know
　How great a woe did us befall.

But as the winter days went by,
　And her dear voice was heard no more,
Nor seen her face, so bright and shy,
　By window or the open door,

Our 'wildered sense to anguish grew:
　Each morning brought a wearier cross:
From all about some spirit flew
　To tell the pathos of our loss.

We longed for her confiding touch,
　The sweet surprises of her speech,

Her wondering look, that meant so much
　　In eyes that love's confessions teach.

We yearned her fair, round cheek to feel,
　　To sit and smooth each soft brown tress,
To have her arms about us steal
　　In speechless, infantile caress.

Again the bright May blossoms spring : —
　　It hurts to see them grow so fair ;
The birds returning soar and sing,
　　Yet dirges seem to pain the air.

The odor of the apple bloom
　　Faints for her sweet and vanished breath ;
The very sunlight in the room
　　Reveals the vacancy of death.

We do not wish the beauty less
　　In aught the gentle season brings,
Though tears start at the loveliness
　　In buds and songs and glancing wings.

But O, how different earth would be,
  And home and life and all things dear
To heart and hope, if only she,
  Just as she used to be, were here!

MATTHEW ARNOLD.

DAZED with the sudden shock I stood,
As if stealthily struck in the dark,
Conscious only of strangeness and pain —
A gnawing and desperate pain,
As I groped in the awful void.
Arnold dead! O soul-searching woe!
The elect of the Muses fled!
Great Voice of the century dumb!
Arnold dead! Lordly pattern of man,
Oracle, charmer of souls,
Compeller of strenuous life,
Revealer of secrets untold,
Consoler, interpreter, friend!

How flock to my vision the shapes
That refresh, enamour, inspire
The children of spirit and light,
Embosomed in blossoms of song.

Fields of royal tillage I see,
And battles and spoils of the mind ;
Himself disembodied I see,
His courage, his clearness, his truth,
His genius serene, unappalled,
His sweetness diffused in the lives
Ennobled, enriched by his own.
How splendid the path of his feet,
His prophecies, music, and power,
The depths and the heights that he trod !

Silent, grieving, alone,
I droop in my study's gloom :
But throngs of the deathless are here —
The immortals untrammeled, unstained,
Who smile at the greed of the grave.
All is life, pure life, that I see,
Exulting, achieving, untired,
Eternal and moving in God —
Yet the mortal presence has fled !
In the instinct of love I arise
And fondle the volumes he penned,

As if I were smoothing the brow
Of the cold, white face of the dead.
The leaves of one fall apart,
Which I kiss in the yearning of pain.
O wonder! O tender decree!
As if pointed out by his hand,
" Resignation " looks up from the page!
Resignation writ for my soul.

And I read and try to be calm.
And opening at random its mate,
Unthinking of aught I may see,
Strange again, " A Wish " first appears,
Breathing calmness, humility, peace.
Thou art speaking in pity to me —
Sweetly thoughtful and tender in death!
But tears are blinding me now,
Yes, " Worse plagues are on earth than
          tears."
And others are weeping, I know,
In gratitude, sorrow, and awe —
The meek, the unselfish, the mild,

Who love not the things of the world,
Who strive for the flawless ideal,
Who mirror the Christ among men.
Hot tears are in eyes that still strain
For the vision of good that endures,
That long for the glorified day.
O the fathomless grief o'er the sea!
Dear home! wife and children and friends
Who loved the great heart that is still.

Who shall chaunt the high theme of his
    life?
Who is left of our age that can fill
The trumpet that honors his muse?
Long ago burning Shelley was mute,
And Byron, the Titan of song;
Young, honey-lipped Keats sits above;
Only Nature breathes Wordsworth's
    refrain.
'Neath his chaplets the Laureate nods
In the affluent ease of his fame.
Will Browning of genius austere

Meetly measure the bard we deplore —
Tell the sweep and the stress of his voice
That thrilled through our cold-hearted
　　　years?

But he stepped into clearer light —
A single step — and he knew
The secrets that baffle us here.
O blessed and beautiful death!
Out, 'neath the open sky,
The spring grass under his feet,
The air like the kiss of a soul,
Saluted by sunshine and birds,
Keeping step with the angel of love,
Joyous, clear-visioned, composed —
Death to him was a rapture of life:
May it so come, in kindness, to me.

ENCOURAGEMENT.

TELL me, O gentle friend, again,
  That He who all our sorrows bore,
Softens thy weary couch of pain
  With peace that deepens more and more.

Tell me, confiding heart secure,
  Like John, upon the Saviour's breast,
That it is love that keeps thee pure,
  And gives thee, mid the tempest, rest.

Tell me, O erring one restored,
  That something strangely gracious drew
Thee out of darkness to the Lord,
  And, henceforth, everything was new.

Tell me, O sore bereaved, whose face
  Is bright mid tears that have to flow,

That One abides whose tender grace
   Consoles and consecrates thy woe.

Tell me, O ye who still maintain,
   Though bruised and scarred, your fight with
      wrong,
That, dying unto self, ye gain
   The power that makes you brave and strong.

Thanks for each faithful witness borne
   Of life made sweet in loss and care,
Of light that shines to those who mourn,
   And all the wondrous lore of prayer.

Precious is every word that shows
   How faith, though tried, may conquer still,
That breathes the blessedness of those
   Who meekly do the Master's will.

Speak, only speak, of what has been
   Thy stay and staff in life's long need,
And thou shalt cheer the hearts of men,
   Though now they ache and faint and
      bleed.

EASTER EVEN.

O WOEFUL day ! but there is day no more —
  The horrid deed of darkness has been done :
Can aught to earth the light of love restore?
  It is not light, though shines the noonday
    sun.

O murdered Master ! Cold sepulchral stone !
  O sky of ashes that is more than gloom !
Closed is the grave : earth and the grave are
    one,
  And all my heart is hollowed to a tomb.

Why could they not their spiteful hate forego?
  He was so beautiful, so good, so grand :
O agony ! to see the red drops flow
  From his fair brow and lacerated hand ;

To see the pallor spread, the quivering frame
　　And its dark welts, gored feet and droop-
　　　　ing head;
To hear Him gasp, at last, the one dear name,
　　And then to know this blessed one was dead.

Where shall I go?   This is no Sabbath rest.
　　'Twould ease me much, I think, if I could
　　　　fold
Some precious balms about his cold still breast,
　　As to my heart his precious Love I hold.

This will I do at morn : His tomb is dear —
　　O haste, slow morn! I cannot bear my
　　　　pain —
But list!   His once mysterious words I hear :
　　" On the third day, and I shall rise again."

Sweet ray of hope! O glimmer in the dark!
　　Prophetic voice that meets the soul's deep
　　　　cries.
Will the light grow from this faint, flickering
　　　　spark?
Will blessed life from cruel death arise?

EASTER.

Sing, heart! I have met Him
   All radiant, victorious!
I have met Him and heard Him —
   The conqueror glorious!
I have seen Him and touched Him —
   He has broken the prison:
It is life, it is light, —
   The Christ has arisen.

O the light after night,
   O the peace after pain,
O my Lord, my delight,
   Forever to reign!
Dear faces are dearer,
   O how sweet is the sun!
Death loses its terror,
   In the life He has won.

In my heart He has risen :
  O the rapture divine !
I am His by His triumph,
  In His love, He is mine.

I am risen, I'm born
  In the love that renews :
This is life's perfect morn,
  I am bathed in its dews.
Vain fears that oppressed me,
  In yesterday's gloom,
Ye cannot molest me,
  With heart all abloom.
What is death?   What its sting?
  The tyrant is slain :
Life is victor and king,
  It is Life that shall reign.

THE PHONOGRAPH'S SALUTATION.

I SEIZE the palpitating air.   I hoard
　　Music and speech.   All lips that speak are
　　　　mine.
I speak, and the inviolable word
　　Authenticates its origin and sign.

I am a tomb, a paradise, a throne,
　　An angel, prophet, slave, immortal friend :
My living records in their native tone
　　Convict the knave and disputations end.

In me are souls embalmed.   I am an ear
　　Flawless as Truth ; and Truth's own tongue
　　　　am I.
I am a resurrection, and men hear
　　The quick and dead converse, as I reply.

Hail, English shores and homes and marts of
 peace !
 Well were your trophies through the ages
 won.
May " sweetness," " light " and brotherhood
 increase !
 I am the youngest born of Edison.

LILIES.

O THE lilies! I've found lilies! they star the
    lovely meadow —

Glorious, great lilies, flakes of light in seas of
    verdure!

Wings of gold and ranks of splendor! stately,
    musing, queenly lilies!

Thoughts of angels writ in petals of velvet
    gleaming bloom!

And the birds are singing o'er them in deli-
    cious summer rapture,

And lustrous sunshine bathes them from the
    delicate blue sky.

O royal vestured lilies! with the gentle Christ
    amongst you,

The dear and perfect Christ amongst you tall
    and fair.

Yes, the Lord has touched, caressed you, and
 breathed your spicy odors,
And His face is toward your beauty with a
 love that makes you glad.
How the birds sing ! How the dew gleams !
 how the soft wind wafts the perfumes
With the faint, low music floating up the
 clover-scented vale !
O the calm and glow of morning, with the
 lilies all a-blossom,
And the Master musing in their midst with
 sweet, unruffled brow !
And companies of people pause beside the
 lilied meadow —
Stern men and little children, eager youths
 and meek-eyed maidens —
And the Christ among the lilies tells of their
 trustful growing,
Of the love that makes them lovely, and a
 Father's tender care.
And some scowl and hurry onward, some
 smile in deep derision,

Some wonder at the folly that can dally with
    a blossom.

There are pale, pinched, pleading faces, and
    hearts that ache and languish ;

As they listen, how hope brightens, how their
    cruel burdens fall !

And children kiss the lilies 'neath the halos
    that o'erspread them,

And virgins see a vision in the bloom that is
    immortal,

And eyes are wet with gladness as some leave
    the barren pathways,

And enter into gardens where no blight of
    evil falls.

O the memories, the awakenings, the solaces,
    thanksgivings,

In the messages that whisper in the paradise
    of lilies,

With the loving Christ among them where the
    fadeless sunlight falls !

O the lilies ! O my lilies ! it is love that tells
    your story —

Love that fills the earth and heavens with the
beauty you reveal.

In your sumptuous summer sweetness I am
bathed with your caresses.

O my lilies! Christ has touched you, He has
breathed and smiled upon you,

He stands among you pleading that the souls
of men be like you,

In the glory of that kingdom where His full-
ness is for all.

SOWING IN THE SEA.

A HAPPY child, with playful glee,
Was casting blossoms on the sea;
O'er heaving wave and flashing spray
The fragrant navy sailed away:
How could the thoughtless urchin know
That in the ocean he could sow?

One branch the slow tides tended o'er,
And planted on a foreign shore.
It grew, a marvelous plant, whose leaf
With healing virtue gave relief
To dire disease and weary pain,
And joy filled many hearts again.

Thus in the world's discordant strife,
Where come and go the waves of life,

And furious passions overflow
The beauteous things that else might grow,
A look of love, a tender speech,
May some sad, aching bosom reach,
And generous deeds and liberal hands
May heal sick souls in distant lands.

THE TRANSFIGURATION.

RESPLENDENT as the sun
Upon the mountain height,
Shines the Anointed One
In raiment dazzling white.
Spirits of Eld appear
In converse with the Lord :
" Good is it to be here,"
Is Peter's rapturous word.
And then a glowing cloud
Wraps awful splendors round,
And messages aloud
From its effulgence sound.
O'erwhelmed with holy dread,
The dazed apostles fall ;
Yet what is seen and said
Is light and life for all.

The Vision and the Voice
Forever beckon on : —
Hear Him, see Him, rejoice
In the Beloved Son.

———

Keep we the Feast.   In whiter robes, to-day,
  O Bride of Christ, devotion's zeal employ ;
A brighter sheen of holiness display,
  And find in larger love illustrious joy.

Ascend, disciple — rise in heart — arise !
  The beauty of the King shall be revealed,
And thou shalt read, with faith's transported
    eyes,
  Great meanings that to sluggish souls are
    sealed.

Go up the mount.   There shines in dimless
    white
  The perfect One, transcendent, all-adored !
The cloud around is an excess of light
  That flows unwasting from the living Lord.

Go up, faint heart.   The sky is clear above ;
  The dark melts slowly at the mountain's
      base.
Go up and watch the promised Day of Love
  Flashing and spreading o'er our groping
      race.

Thou shalt see marvels — soul-births, amities,
  Balms that refresh and heal the world's wild
      strife,
And tender trusts and gracious charities
  That make so beautiful our daily life.

Thou shalt commune with spirit that resides
  In all that is, in earth and sky and sea,
And feel secure, though round thee sweep the
      tides
  Of an abysmal, dark eternity.

Go up, go up ! " 'tis the Beloved Son !
  Hear Him ! " cry heaven-persuading voices
      sweet.

O rapture! When the glorious heights are
    won,
  Dominions, Thrones, and Powers are at His
    feet.

Transfigured and enamored! All who give
  Themselves for man and steeps of duty
    climb,
And for the Truth's dear sake, die while they
    live,
  Meet with the Master on the mount sublime.

O blessed company! adoring throng!
  Awe-smitten, prostrate, and yet raised to
    know
A grander Vision, and to grow more strong
  In Him who leads in paths they love to go.

WHITSUN-DAY.

LOVE's great illumination!   O the joy in love
     and light!
  How the glory streams and brightens!
  How the light of love enlightens!
What baleful phantoms vanish with the pass-
     ing of the night!

Creation new-created!   O the beauty rare and
     sweet!
  Hear the hallelujahs tender!
  See the rapturous surrender
Of hearts that fling the flowers of life before
     the Master's feet!

Tongues of fire in truth and blessing!   O
     trumpet tones and meek!
  Swiftly speeds the message holy;

How it cheers the poor and lowly!
How nations catch the tidings that exulting
    spirits speak!

What prophecies! confessions! O travelers
    lone and sad,
  Lift your weary heads and listen!
  How the love-lit faces glisten,
As praises break from prisons and the desert-
    ways are glad.

Woven amaranths and lilies! O miracle of
    white!
  O the lives where they are growing!
  O the loveliness they're sowing,
As duty and devotion breathe their odors of
    delight!

See the kindness, the forgiving, the rescues,
    the relief;
  With what power the Word is spoken!
  Where a heart is hurt or broken,
What cordial for the fainting, and what pre-
    cious balm for grief!

O the courage, knowledge, wisdom, in man's
    divine release !
  Longing eyes no more are holden,
  All the centuries are golden,
The cruel sheathe their weapons and earth's
    maddening discords cease.

WINTERGREEN.

TO J. D.

DID you not know that many a fateful year
  Had shrunk her cheek and seamed her
    snowy brow,
Did you not see her face, but only hear
  Her blithesome accents as I hear them now;

Did you but feel her charm, while unaware
  Of time's invasion, you would fain suppose
She was a creature unassailed by care,
  And glowing yet with life's unwithered rose.

But though, long since, she hailed her three-
    score-ten,
  The wonder is no less that she can wear
The jewels of her loveliness, as when
  The gold of youth was gleaming in her hair.

Children are poems to her : songs of spring
  With all the rapture of old days are heard,
And grateful memories of her pleasures sing
  In tender chorus with the sweetest bird.

She loves the glorious landscape spread
        around
  With the deep passion of her beauteous May ;
Sorrows that cloud the world and wrongs that
        wound,
  Have frightened not her generous trusts
  away.

The mourner's cup she shares, as 'twere her
        own,
  Delights in all the noblest bards have sung.
Love's accents reach her to their faintest tone,
  And love's own music vibrates on her
  tongue.

In all that gladdens others she is glad ;
  She gives the key to household converse
  sweet,

Translates to cheerful meaning tidings sad,
　And feels in all the pulse of goodness beat.

And so the verdure of her life remains,
　In spite of frosts that bite and winds that
　　blow ;
The heart of youth is throbbing in her veins,
　The flowers and fruitage mingle 'neath the
　　snow.

UNDERTONES.

"Heard melodies are sweet, but those unheard
Are sweeter." — KEATS.

A LOW and witching strain —
  Far off, but strangely near:
It dies, and wakes, and breathes again
  To my enchanted ear.

Is it to sense alone
  The subtle sound appeals?
A spirit in its undertone
  Another world reveals.

Far through the trembling blue
  The mystic accents come,
As if they told in numbers new
  The sweetest dream of home.

And yet from shrub and tree,
   And blossoms' dewy bell,
And singing bird and droning bee,
   The fairy rondeaux swell.

I cannot help but hear —
   So sweet, so pure it seems,
Like voice of one surpassing dear
   Who breathes her love in dreams.

Ah, it is Nature's heart
   With its own rapture stirred !
And blest is he whose cunning art
   Translates her loving word.

JUNE.

O LUSCIOUS June ! O perfect Flower !
Pure Pearl of Summer's regal dower !
Soul of the Seasons ! Eden's sign !
Goblet of Beauty's sacred wine !
Music and love are born of thee —
Essence of Nature's ecstasy !

Imperial June ! with laughing eyes
From beds of bloom, I see thee rise.
I see the fairy forms that dress
Thy unimagined loveliness —
Thy scarfs of light, thy glowing zone,
Thy locks on scented breezes blown,
Thy airy step, caressing grace,
Dimples and sunshine of thy face.

And ah, by thee what tales are told
Writ only in thy book of gold !

I hear the gossip in the grass,
And love-sighs as the zephyrs pass,
The daisy's kiss where lilies lean
With tempting cheek and royal sheen,
And strawberries blushing coyly tell
How all their nectared juices swell.
I hear what bridal roses say
To maidens at the close of day,
When all the witchery of the hour
Distills its sweetness in the flower;
And what is told by whispering sedge
In star-shine by the lakelet's edge,
The thrush's converse in the woods
About the prayerful solitudes,
The brooklet's secret, and the tone
Heard when the soul is most alone.
Ah, June! what prophecies are thine —
Teasing, unutterable, divine!

I feel the Spirit that impels
All impulse — all that works and dwells
In mystic germ and hidden cell

Of life's deep, dateless miracle;
The living energy I feel
That turns unmeasured Nature's wheel,—
The Soul that breathes in life and law
From which all truth and beauty draw
The power to touch our finest sense
With Love's benign omnipotence.

LIGHT AT EVENTIDE.

I DID not think in other days,
    Musing on life's decline,
Amid the dark and thorny ways
    That had so long been mine,

That after weary years at length
    My chain would fall apart,
And I should gather up my strength
    With uncorroded heart;

That here my youth would be renewed,
    My broken hearthstone rise,
And life again grow rosy-hued
    To my confiding eyes;

And noble spirits flow to mine
    In friendship large and free,

And all that's sweet and true and fine
   Be here reserved for me.

How rich the portion that I share,
   Though tearfully I've sown !
A recompense comes unaware
   While seeking not my own.

I ramble o'er these hills, and feel,
   As charm on charm invites,
That none can seize my wealth, nor steal
   The spice of my delights.

Dear eyes look into mine, and beam
   With sympathy untold,
I verify the golden dream
   That haunted me of old.

In God's great temple I adore
   With wonderment and awe
The Love whose miracle is more
   Than prophet ever saw.

And the dear Christ whose sacred feet
   Guide where still water flows
Leads me in pastures green and sweet
   To a divine repose.

O tranquil rest! O heart serene!
   Contented I abide :
However dark my day has been,
   Light crowns its eventide.

BEHIND THE VEIL.

As I muse in the hush of evening,
   Between the day and the night,
A veil is sometimes lifted
   That hides the common sight,
And scenes of time and the senses
   Utterly fade away,
And I see what I can never see
   In the glare of open day.

There are pictures of landscapes fairer
   Than any the masters paint,
There are mounts of splendid vision
   Ne'er reached by purest saint,
There are trophies of grander triumph
   Than of kings of old renown,
And the garlands the victors gather
   Are more than a triple crown.

I have glimpses of sweetest creatures
　On gracious service bound,
Whose unimagined beauty
　On earth no mortal found :
Beings whose radiant spirit
　Envelops form and face
With a glory whose mere reflection
　Is a sacrament of grace.

I see the heights of honor
　That no man yet has trod
And awful gleams, like splendors
　About the feet of God ;
I see where hands are lifted
　And brows are bathed in light
And angels hush their music
　And stop in their eager flight.

I see the untold marvels
　Of being's utmost reach,
When mind has made the conquest.
　That all the ages preach ;

The miracle and harvest
  Of life's supremest gain,
When truth is loved for what it is
  And wrong and error slain.

I look through glowing vistas
  Resplendent, without end,
Where voices of all time and space
  In one great chorus blend:
And in the vision of the good
  That is the sun of all,
As in a boundless sea of love,
  Instinctively I fall.

www.ingramcontent.com/pod-product-compliance
Lightning Source LLC
Chambersburg PA
CBHW030552270326
41927CB00008B/1618